AF408412

Mousekin's Twelve Days of Christmas

Written and illustrated by
Nancy Arny Pi-Sunyer

Acknowledgments

Thanks to Mousekin's many friends and fans who have encouraged me over the years it has taken to bring Mousekin and his infectious smile to many new readers, including YOU.

Special thanks to family, friends and mentors including (but not limited to)
Luis C. Pi-Sunyer, Jon and Jen Pywell, Patricia Park Connell, Stephanie Haas,
Gunta Alexander and Lynn Salehi.

Thanks also to Henry H. Neff and Lauren Koueiter who guided me through
the redesign of Mousekin's first official publication.

Published by NARNY Productions
149 Watchung Avenue, Montclair, NJ 07043-1712

ISBN 979-8-9892350-0-1

Book design by Lauren Koueiter
Printed in the United States of America by Ingram Spark

*This book is dedicated to my husband,
Luis C. Pi-Sunyer,
with eternal thanks for becoming my partner
and my greatest cheerleader.*

Hand in hand may we continue down life's road.

On the first day of Christmas, Mousekin showed
me a European partridge in a pear tree.

Unusual, as they normally feed on the ground.

On the second day of Christmas, Mousekin introduced me to two turtle doves.

They are checking out an English holly tree (and each other)!

The third day of Christmas, Mousekin
and three French hens hung out together
under the Christmas tree.

Rowan berries, like Mousekin, are covered with ice and snow **on the fourth day of Christmas.** They make good food for the colly birds. (That's "coaly" like "black as coal".)

On the fifth day of Christmas, Mousekin flushed
five golden ring-necked pheasants. Have you noticed
it's birds again? Some folks think this verse is about
jewelry rings. That makes no sense to the story!

Mousekin was surprised, ***on the sixth day of Christmas,*** to find six geese laying eggs. This is not usual in December, but it can certainly happen. February to April is more usual egg-laying time.

On the seventh day of Christmas, Mousekin spied
seven swans swimming in the lake.

In Scotland, they call lakes "lochs."
Aren't the swans lovely?

On the eighth day of Christmas, Mousekin visited the milkmaids who were collecting milk to make custards, butter and other goodies for the Twelfth Night feast.

It's the ninth day of Christmas and Mousekin
is helping nine ladies to choreograph their dance
for the festival. Mousekin is hoping someday to see
a mouse in a ballet. Maybe even a Mouse King!
He wonders if that could ever happen.

It's the tenth day of Christmas. Lords are leaping, practicing a fortune-telling game. Jumping the candle without blowing out the flame is supposed to bring good luck in the New Year.

It's the eleventh day of Christmas. Mousekin is
among eleven bagpipers practicing for tomorrow.
Robert Burns could write a poem to this handsome
little critter in his Lamont tartan.

It's Twelfth Night! Mousekin is one of twelve
drummers welcoming the holiday.

Mousekin has counted down to *Twelfth Night*
and it is time for the festivities to begin. Lords
and ladies will gather around the table for a feast.
There will be music and dancing, games and
gifts. It will be a late night for sleepy young mice.

Twelfth Night Traditions

A favorite dessert is three kings cake. Mouskin learned from the baker that the cake may have a dried bean baked into it. The person who gets the slice of cake with the bean is crowned King for the Twelfth Night party. Some bakers use a tiny charm in the shape of a baby Jesus.

Family and friends gather at the party to play games like jumping over a lit candle to see if they will have good luck in the New Year. They might also play a memory-and-forfeit game. In this game one person sings the first line of the song and the next player must sing the first and add the second line. Each player adds another line to the song.

If a player doesn't remember the words, he or she has to give the last player a kiss or some small token to pay for their forgetfulness.

So you and Mousekin's other friends will not have to pay a forfeit, on the following pages you will find the words of the song as we sing it today.

21ˢᵗ-Century Song Lyrics

On the first day of Christmas my true love gave to me a partridge in a pear tree.

On the second day of Christmas my true love gave to me, two turtle doves and a partridge in a pear tree.

On the third day of Christmas my true love gave to me three French hens, two turtle doves and a partridge in a pear tree.

On the fourth day of Christmas my true love gave to me four calling birds, three French hens, two turtle doves and a partridge in a pear tree.

On the fifth day of Christmas my true love gave to me five golden rings, four calling birds, three French hens, two turtle doves and a partridge in a pear tree.

On the sixth day of Christmas my true love gave to me six geese a-laying,

five golden rings, four calling birds, three French hens, two turtle doves and a partridge in a pear tree.

On the seventh day of Christmas my true love gave to me seven swans a-swimming, six geese a-laying, five golden rings, four calling birds, three French hens, two turtle doves and a partridge in a pear tree.

On the eighth day of Christmas my true love gave to me eight maids a-milking, seven swans a-swimming, six geese a-laying, five golden rings, four calling birds, three French hens, two turtle doves and a partridge in a pear tree.

On the ninth day of Christmas my true love gave to me nine ladies dancing, eight maids a-milking, seven swans a-swimming, six geese a-laying, five golden rings, four calling birds, three French hens, two turtle doves and a partridge in a pear tree.

On the tenth day of Christmas my true love gave to me ten lords a-leaping, nine ladies dancing, eight maids a-milking, seven swans a-swimming, six geese a-laying, five golden rings, four calling birds, three French hens, two turtle doves and a partridge in a pear tree.

On the eleventh day of Christmas my true love gave to me eleven pipers piping, ten lords a-leaping, nine ladies dancing, eight maids a-milking, seven swans a-swimming, six geese a-laying, five

golden rings, four calling birds, three French hens, two turtle doves and a partridge in a pear tree.

On the twelfth day of Christmas my true love gave to me twelve drummers drumming, eleven pipers piping, ten lords a-leaping, nine ladies dancing, eight maids a-milking, seven swans a-swimming, six geese a-laying, five golden rings, four calling birds, three French hens, two turtle doves and a partridge in a pear tree.

Mousekin Knows...

...Gift Giving used to be done on Twelfth Night. Mousekin knows that the very first Christmas gifts were from the three wise men, also known as magi or kings. They brought gold and frankincense and myrrh to the baby Jesus in the stable where he was born.

...January sixth is the eve of Epiphany, the day the three wise men arrived to worship baby Jesus in Bethlehem. It is twelve days after Christmas on December 25th.

...There is an old Scottish poem called "The Yule Days" that tells of a king who gave his lady gifts including a partridge, geese, swans and black birds called starlings. Mousekin is pretty sure this is where some of the words for "The Twelve Days of Christmas" came from.

...The words we sing now were first printed in a book in England in 1780. This children's book called *Mirth Without Mischief* included the words as a poem. In 1909 Fredrich Austin, an English singer and composer, wrote the tune we sing.

...There is a rumor that the song was a Church School lesson in a secret code. Mousekin knows this is not true. Another myth is that it's all about birds. You can see that it is really all about Twelfth Night: the food, the games, and the gifts.

... Instead of the gifts the three wise men brought, Mousekin chooses to bring Peace, Joy and Love to the holiday and to the year ahead.

Christmas has come to an end once more. It's Twelfth Night and it is time to undo the tree and put away the trappings and wrappings of Christmas 'til next year.

But don't pack away the Joy, Peace and Love this season has brought. Keep Christmas in your heart all year long.

Love,
Mousekin

About The Author/Illustrator

Nature is my inspiration. Since my earliest childhood days in Montclair, New Jersey, the wonders and beauty of the natural world have been integral to my personal life, my professional life and my artistic expression.

Since my Children's Literature class in my undergraduate days at Boston University, I have had the dream of writing, illustrating and publishing a children's book. I am happy to share my dream with you and I hope that my readers will enjoy this product of my latest career. Mousekin is injecting a lot of energy and activity into my "retirement years".

For more information, please visit Pi-SunyerNaturally.com